mini ENCYCLOPEDIA

WEATHER

D0398409

Contents

What is weather?

Wind, clouds, sunshine, rain, hail, snow, fog, mist, and frost make up our weather from day to day. At times, the weather is freezing cold; at others, it is scorching hot. On some days, there are winds and storms, while on others, it is cloudless and calm. To measure our weather, we use a number of different instruments.

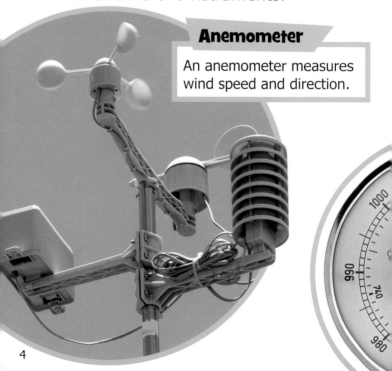

Anemometer

An anemometer measures wind speed and direction.

2.0

1.0

0.5

IN.

Rain gauge

A rain gauge measures the amount of rain that falls.

Thermometer

A double-ended thermometer records the maximum and minimum temperatures each day.

Min   Max

Barometer

A barometer measures the pressure of the air. Low pressure often means there will be wind and rain.

5

Climate and seasons

The overall weather pattern in a place is known as its climate. Climate depends on how far north or south a place is, whether it is in the middle of a continent or by the ocean, and whether it is a low-lying plain or a high mountain valley.

Deciduous forests grow well here. The summers are warm, the winters mild, and there is plenty of rain.

Seasons

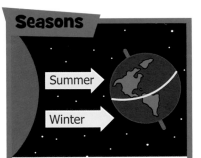

Summer

Winter

The tilt of the Earth as it travels around the Sun causes seasons. It is winter in the part tilting away from the Sun and summer in the part tilting towards the Sun.

In deserts, the weather is hot and dry all year round. Only cacti can survive.

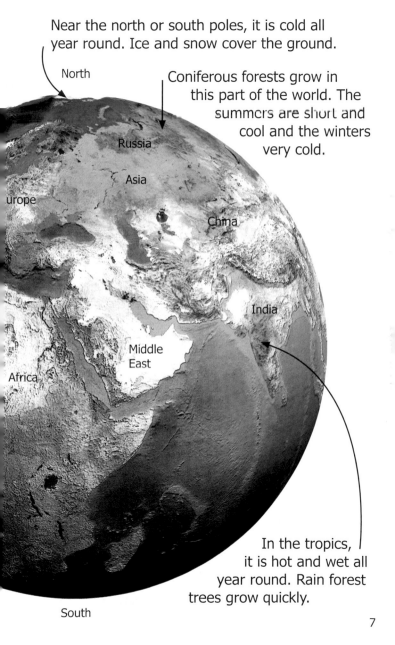

Near the north or south poles, it is cold all year round. Ice and snow cover the ground.

North

Coniferous forests grow in this part of the world. The summers are short and cool and the winters very cold.

Russia

Asia

Europe

China

India

Middle East

Africa

In the tropics, it is hot and wet all year round. Rain forest trees grow quickly.

South

7

Clouds

Air contains invisible water vapor. As the air rises, it cools, and some of the water vapor turns into tiny droplets of water, or freezes to form ice. The water droplets or bits of ice form clouds. When air rises slowly, sheets of cloud form. When air rises quickly, the water and ice form separate clumps of cloud.

Altocumulus clouds are small and puffy. They form between 6,500 and 20,000 ft (2,000–6,000 m).

Nimbostratus clouds are thick rain clouds.

Stratus clouds are low and gray and form below 1,300 ft (400 m).

Airplane trails

When airplanes are flying high in the sky, the water vapor from the engine freezes immediately, leaving a trail of cloud across the sky.

Cumulonimbus clouds start below 3,300 ft (1,000 m) but can reach to more than 33,000 ft (10,000 m).

Cumulonimbus clouds can bring thunderstorms.

Wispy cirrus clouds form high in the sky, between 20,000 and 46,000 ft (6,000–14,000 m). They contain only ice.

Altostratus clouds are sheet clouds.

Stratocumulus are lumpy, gray clouds.

White, fluffy cumulus clouds form between 1,500 and 5,000 ft (500–1,500 m).

9

The water cycle

The water falling in rain, sleet, snow, or hail is part of the water cycle. Every day, about 295 billion tons (300 billion tonnes) of rain, sleet, snow, and hail fall on the Earth.

Rain and snow fall on the mountains and hills.

Streams and rivers form.

Did you know?

Almost all rain starts off as snow, even in summer, but the snowflakes melt into raindrops before they reach the ground. Only in cold weather do the flakes reach the ground as snow.

Sometimes water flows under the ground.

The minuscule water droplets that form a cloud bang together and form bigger droplets. When they are big and heavy enough, the droplets fall as rain.

Warm air rises and cools. As it cools, the water vapor that is in the air turns into tiny droplets of water, forming a cloud.

In the warmth of the Sun, water from the sea and the land heats and turns into water vapor.

The wind causes water to evaporate from lakes and oceans.

Water vapor passes from the leaves of trees out into the air.

Winds

Winds are large blocks of air that move because of the Sun's heat. When the Sun heats an area of air, it becomes lighter and rises. Cold air flows in to take its place, and it is this movement of air that creates wind.

Sea and land breezes

During the day, the land heats up quickly. The air above the land warms and rises and cool air flows in from the sea. At night, the sea loses heat more slowly. The air above it rises and cool air blows out from the land.

The strength of the wind turns the blades. ——

A generator in this part —— of the turbine changes the movement of the blades into electricity.

The tower holds the blades high in the air, where the wind is stronger. ——

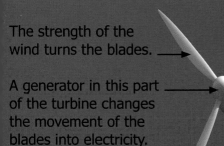

Wind power

Wind turbines turn the power of the wind into electricity.

Forecasting weather

The scientists who study the weather are known as meteorologists. They produce forecasts so that we know what weather to expect. Images of the Earth taken from satellites provide lots of useful information.

CloudSat

South America

A satellite's view

Weather satellites are specially designed machines that are launched into space. They send back pictures of clouds and lots of other information about our weather.

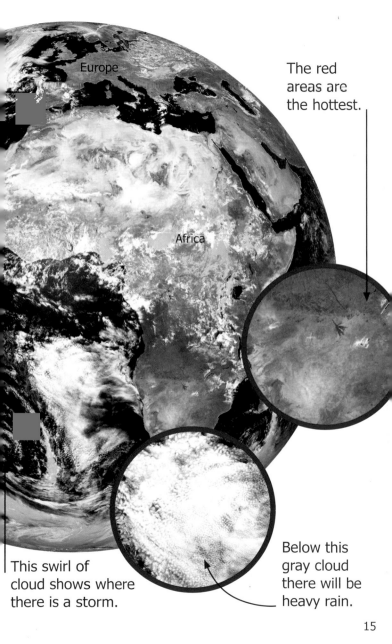

Europe

The red
areas are
the hottest.

Africa

This swirl of
cloud shows where
there is a storm.

Below this
gray cloud
there will be
heavy rain.

15

Weather charts

Meteorologists produce charts that record the weather and show what they think it will be like over the next few days.

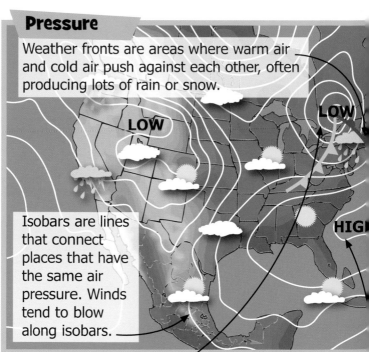

Pressure

Weather fronts are areas where warm air and cold air push against each other, often producing lots of rain or snow.

LOW

LOW

HIGH

Isobars are lines that connect places that have the same air pressure. Winds tend to blow along isobars.

An area of low pressure is called a low or a cyclone. It is an area where air is rising, often producing cloud, wind, and rain.

A region of high pressure is known as a high or an anticyclone. It is an area where the air is pressing down and usually brings calm, settled weather.

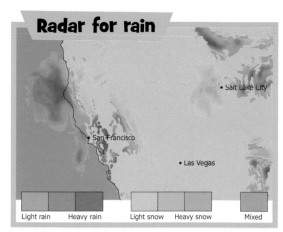

Radar for rain

| Light rain | Heavy rain | Light snow | Heavy snow | Mixed |

Radar sees which clouds contain rain or snow. Radar pictures show where rain or snow is falling and how heavy it is.

Hot or cold?

50 Vancouver
23 Winnipeg
43 Montreal
54 San Francisco
54 Chicago
70 New York
61 Los Angeles
82 Dallas
79 Miami
90 Monterrey
84 Havana
°Fahrenheit

Temperature maps show which places are hot and which are cold. The yellow area is warm, the green area is cooler, the blue is cooler again, and the purple is the coolest of all.

17

Global warming

Water, carbon dioxide, and methane all trap heat around the Earth. We produce lots of carbon dioxide as we use gasoline to power our cars and oil or gas to heat our houses. Almost all weather experts believe these gases are causing the Earth to warm up.

Carbon dioxide

A traffic jam in the US.

Methane

We farm lots of animals for meat. As they digest their food, the animals produce methane gas, which is causing the Earth to get warmer.

Water

As the Earth heats up, the ice at the poles is melting, so that there is a lot more water in the seas. In years to come, rising sea levels will make it very difficult to live on many islands and areas near the sea.

Thunder and lightning

When lots of warm, wet air rises quickly, it cools and forms thunderclouds. Some of the water in the clouds freezes to form hail and snow. The ice bangs together in the strong winds and creates an electrical charge, which we see as flashes of lightning. The lightning heats the air around it, making it expand faster than the speed of sound. We hear this as a crash of thunder.

Lightning speed

If a storm is overhead, you see the lightning and hear the thunder at the same time. But if it is some distance away, you will see the lightning first and hear the thunder later. This is because light travels faster than sound.

High winds blow the top of the cloud.

The cloud is full of ice and water.

Forked lightning zigzags to the ground.

Forks or sheets?

Forked lightning shoots down to the ground, whereas sheet lightning flashes from one point to another within the storm cloud.

Tornadoes

Tornadoes, sometimes known as twisters, are spinning columns of air. They form beneath huge cumulonimbus storm clouds when cool, dry air collides with warm, moist air. Tornadoes can destroy buildings and pull up trees.

The tornado is a spinning column of air that stretches down from the cloud to the ground.

The tornado picks up things from the ground and pulls them high into the air.

The winds in a tornado are the fastest on Earth – they reach speeds of 280 mph (450 kph).

Waterspout

When a tornado forms over the ocean, the winds can suck up a huge tower of water. The waterspout can be as tall as 328 ft (100 m).

Hurricanes

Hurricanes are violent, tropical storms. They form over warm seas, as vast quantities of water evaporate. The warm, wet air rises quickly and forms huge cumulonimbus storm clouds. The winds in a hurricane can be as fast as 200 mph (320 kph).

Seen from space, a hurricane looks like a whirlpool of cloud. ⟶

Strong winds at the top of the storm cause bands of swirling cloud. ⟶

The thick clouds cause heavy rain.

In different parts of the world, hurricanes are known as tropical cyclones and typhoons. In Australia, people sometimes call them Willy-Willies!

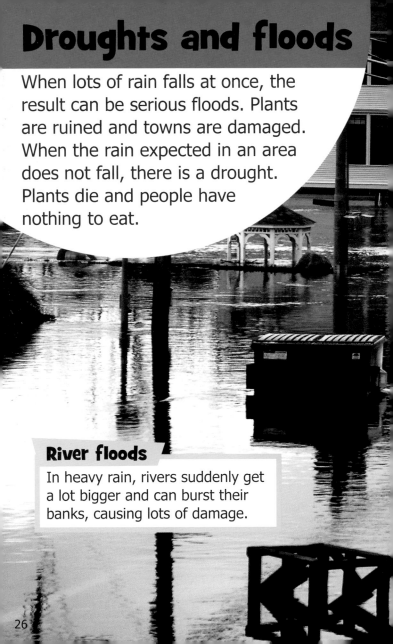

Droughts and floods

When lots of rain falls at once, the result can be serious floods. Plants are ruined and towns are damaged. When the rain expected in an area does not fall, there is a drought. Plants die and people have nothing to eat.

River floods

In heavy rain, rivers suddenly get a lot bigger and can burst their banks, causing lots of damage.

Dry as dust

Deserts are areas that receive little or no rain. Some are hot, but others are cold. The Sahara is the biggest hot desert in the world.

Ice and snow

When it is cold, water droplets freeze to form tiny ice crystals. These collide and join together to form snowflakes. Snowflakes are symmetrical, with six sides. No two snowflakes are the same.

Hail

Hailstones are frozen water droplets that gradually get bigger and bigger as the wind carries them up and down a storm cloud.

Usually the size of small peas, hailstones can occasionally be as big as oranges.

Freezing rain

In ice storms, freezing rain coats everything in a layer of ice that can be 6 in (15 cm) thick! The heavy weight of the ice can pull down electricity cables, causing power cuts.

Frost

Frost forms in cold, still weather when the water in the air freezes onto trees, plants, and pavements.

Glossary

This glossary explains some of the harder words in the book.

climate The usual weather in a place.

cloud A white or gray area of tiny water droplets, or pieces of ice. Rain, hail, and snow fall from clouds.

cold front An area where cold air is replacing warm air, often causing rain or snow.

coniferous A tree that produces pine cones. Coniferous trees stay green all year round as they gradually drop and replace their leaves a few at a time.

continent One of the Earth's very large areas of land.

deciduous A tree or shrub that loses its leaves each winter.

drought A long period of time when there is little or no rain.

flood When land that is normally dry gets covered with water.

fog Water droplets just like cloud, but sitting on the ground. Fog makes it hard to see clearly.

frost Small bits of ice that form on trees or other objects that are outside in cold weather.

global warming The warming of the Earth, caused by gases that trap the Earth's heat, stopping it from escaping into space.

hail Small balls of ice that fall from tall cumulonimbus clouds.

hurricane A violent storm with heavy rains and strong winds.

mist A mass of tiny water droplets near to the ground. Mist is not as thick as fog.

ocean A very large area of sea.

radar A system that uses radio waves to work out where objects are. Radar shows us how much snow or rain different clouds contain.

rain Drops of water falling from clouds.

season A period of time with particular weather. In the northern and southern regions of the Earth, there are four seasons each year (spring, summer, fall, and winter). Near the equator, some regions have only two seasons: rainy or dry.

snow Small crystals of ice. Snowflakes are symmetrical and have six sides.

storm Violent weather, with strong winds, rain, hail, or snow, and possibly thunder and lightning.

warm front An area where warm air is replacing colder air, often causing rain or snow.

water cycle The circulation of water on the Earth, as it evaporates from seas into the air, cools to form clouds, falls as rain, and is carried by rivers back out to sea.

water vapor Water in the form of an invisible gas in the air.

wind A block of air that moves.